Art Revelations

Elaine Ward

OLD TESTAMENT

WOMEN

ENCHANTED LION BOOKS
NEW YORK

First American Edition published in 2004 by
Enchanted Lion Books
115 West 18th Street, New York, NY, 10011
Copyright © 2004 McRae Books Srl

Printed and bound in Belgium
A CIP record for this book is available from the Library of Congress

ISBN 1-59270-011-X

The series "Art Revelations"
was created and produced by McRae Books Srl
Borgo Santa Croce, 8 – Florence (Italy)
info@mcraebooks.com

Art History consultant: Roberto Carvalho de Magalhães
Text: Elaine Ward
Illustrations: Studio Stalio (Alessandro Cantucci,
Fabiano Fabbrucci, Andrea Morandi)
Graphic Design: Marco Nardi
Picture Research and editing: Loredana Agosta
Layout: Studio Yotto

opposite: HIERONYMOUS BOSCH,
The Haywain Triptych (left panel), Prado, Madrid

above: SANDRO BOTTICELLI,
Judith, Uffizi Gallery, Florence

previous page:
MATTHIAS STOM,
Samson and Delilah, Galleria Nazionale d'Arte Antica, Rome

ontents

Introduction

A woman of noble character who can find?
She is worth far more than rubies....
She is clothed with strength and dignity
She can laugh at the days to come
She speaks with wisdom
And faithful instruction is on her tongue
She watches over the affairs of her household
and does not eat the bread of idleness.
Her children arise and call her blessed;
Her husband also, and he praises her...
Proverbs 31:10–28

The stories in the Old Testament, or Hebrew Bible, refer to events that took place in the Near East more than 2,000 years ago. At that time society was controled mainly by men and women were expected to be obedient daughters, then loving wives and mothers. Even so, these books of the Bible refer to about 150 women by name. Many of these women lived full and eventful lives and some achieved great wisdom, happiness, or power.

In this illustration the loyal and hard-working Ruth can be seen kneeling before her future husband, Boaz.

DAUNTLESS MOTHERS OF ISRAEL

Many Old Testament mothers not only protected and saved the lives of their children, but were also determining forces in the history of the Jewish people. Jochebed, who gave up her son Moses by placing him in a reed basket on the Nile River, not only saved his life, but also provided the Hebrews with a leader who would free them from slavery (see pp. 14–15). Sarah (see pp. 8–9), Rebekah, (see pp. 10–11), and Bathsheba (see pp. 22–23) all intervened on their son's behalves to ensure they would achieve power according to God's wishes.

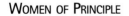

In this detail from a painting by Lucas Cranach the Elder (1472–1553) Eve, the first woman, is shown standing naked in the Garden of Eden before tempting Adam with the forbidden fruit of the Tree of Knowledge.

VIRTUE OR VICE

Many works of art depicting women in the Bible reflect traditional readings of the scripture in which women are often seen as either virtuous and good or very bad. Thus Eve is often shown as a temptress who caused Adam's downfall (see pp. 6–7). Delilah, who revealed the secret of Samson's strength to her people the Philistines, (see pp. 18–19), is usually shown standing, scissors in hand, over Samson as he sleeps. From a Philistine point of view, she was a heroine.

Rebekah gives Abraham's servant, Eliezer, water in this painting by Bartolomé Esteban Murillo (1617–82), the most popular religious painter of the Spanish Baroque.

WOMEN OF PRINCIPLE

Some Old Testament women, such as Ruth, Leah, and Susanna, are known for their loyalty and strong moral principles. Ruth refused to abandon her mother-in-law, Naomi, and accompanied her back to her homeland (see pp. 20–21). Leah was the elder daughter of Laban whose loyalty to her father was shown by her willingness to allow her father to trick Jacob into marrying her instead of her sister, Rachel (see pp. 12–13). Susanna was a virtuous and innocent wife who was falsely accused of adultery and then had to face the humiliation of a public trial (see pp. 26–27).

QUEENS AND HEROINES

Several women in the Old Testament act with great bravery. Most notably, Esther, Jael, and Judith endanger their own lives in order to save the lives of the Israelites, or Hebrews. Jael and Judith both confronted dangerous men on their own (see pp. 16–17 and 26–27), while Esther boldly confronted her husband, the king, to save her people from an evil plot. There are also wealthy, wise, and powerful women such as Deborah the Judge, who led Israel to victory, and the Queen of Sheba, who traveled afar to meet the wise King Solomon (see pp. 24–25).

ESTHER BEFORE AHASUERUS
Konrad Witz
1435–38
Kunstmuseum, Basel (Switzerland)

Konrad Witz (1400–1444) of the Swiss school painted this panel which was once part of the now dismembered Heilspiegel Altarpiece. It shows the crowned Esther (1) as she bows before King Ahasuerus (2), who gives her his blessing with his staff (3). Ahasuerus also holds a golden orb in his left hand (4), which symbolizes his kingship. Their names (5 and 6), written in Gothic letters, appear on either side of the panel. Both figures, dressed in medieval costume, stand before a curtain made of gold with filigree ornamentation (7), typical of altarpieces of the 14th and 15th century. The rich colors used to depict the figures' clothing and the forms of the figures are enhanced by this gold background. The figures seem to come out toward the viewer from the flat picture surface.

Eve

So God created man in his own image,
in the image of God he created him;
male and female he created them. Genesis 1:27

The Bible begins with the book of Genesis which describes how God created the heavens and earth and every living creature. In the first part of the creation story, in Genesis 1, man and woman are created together, in the image of God, and are both given command over every living thing. But in Genesis 2, we are told that God created Adam first and then molded Eve from Adam's rib to be a companion for him. Whatever the case, the Bible is clear about the next part of the story, after God placed Adam and Eve in the Garden of Eden. It is the woman, Eve, "the mother of all the living," who is tempted by the trickster snake into tasting the forbidden fruit from the Tree of Knowledge and who offers the apple to Adam.

This 12th-century relief carving from Autun in France, shows Eve as she reaches out to seize the apple.

THE EXPULSION FROM THE GARDEN OF EDEN

Because Eve disobeyed God's command, she and Adam were expelled from the Garden of Eden. Adam was condemned to toil as a farmer and Eve to painful childbearing and to being ruled over by Adam. In traditional readings of this part of Genesis Eve, like Pandora who opened the box of all evils in the Greek myth, was seen as the one who caused the "Fall of Man." Many modern readers have chosen instead to emphasize Eve's curiosity and her desire to obtain knowledge and wisdom. Eve acted on her own initiative in believing the snake and sampling the fruit; Adam acted passively in eating it although he knew that it was forbidden. It was Eve who changed the order of things and who caused humankind to know good and evil.

An engraving showing Adam, Eve, Cain, and Abel. After they ate the fruit they both became mortal. Adam's punishment was to have to work in the fields until the day he died and Eve was condemned to painful childbearing and to being ruled over by Adam.

THE HAYWAIN TRIPTYCH (left panel)
Hieronymous Bosch
c. 1510
Prado, Madrid (Spain)

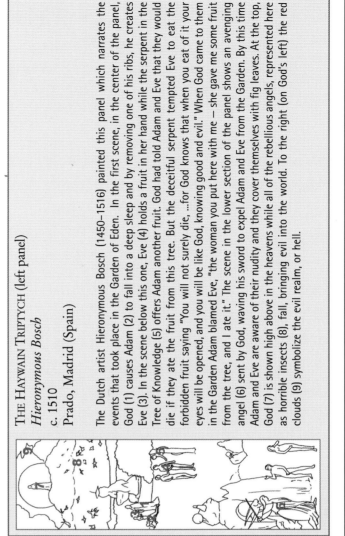

The Dutch artist Hieronymous Bosch (1450–1516) painted this panel which narrates the events that took place in the Garden of Eden. In the first scene, in the center of the panel, God (1) causes Adam (2) to fall into a deep sleep and by removing one of his ribs, he creates Eve (3). In the scene below this one, Eve (4) holds a fruit in her hand while the serpent in the Tree of Knowledge (5) offers Adam another fruit. God had told Adam and Eve that they would die if they ate the fruit from this tree. But the deceitful serpent tempted Eve to eat the forbidden fruit saying "You will not surely die, ...for God knows that when you eat of it your eyes will be opened, and you will be like God, knowing good and evil." When God came to them in the Garden Adam blamed Eve, "the woman you put here with me — she gave me some fruit from the tree, and I ate it." The scene in the lower section of the panel shows an avenging angel (6) sent by God, waving his sword to expel Adam and Eve from the Garden. By this time Adam and Eve are aware of their nudity and they cover themselves with fig leaves. At the top, God (7) is shown high above in the heavens while all of the rebellious angels, represented here as horrible insects (8), fall, bringing evil into the world. To the right (on God's left) the red clouds (9) symbolize the evil realm, or hell.

Sarah and Hagar

God also said to Abraham, "As for Sarai your wife, you are no longer to call her Sarai; her name will be Sarah. I will bless her and will surely give you a son by her. I will bless her so that she will be the mother of nations; kings of people will come from her."   Genesis 17:15-16

Sarah and Hagar both played key roles in the life of Abraham, the founding father of the Hebrew nation. Sarah was Abraham's wife. After many years of marriage without having children, she gave her Egyptian servant, Hagar, to Abraham so that a son could be born. Hagar gave birth to Ishmael. When Sarah finally gave birth to Isaac relations between the two women deteriorated, and Sarah banished Hagar and Ishmael to the desert. Sarah's son Isaac was the second patriarch and father of Jacob.

This detail of a fresco by Italian artist Giovanni Battista Tiepolo (1696–1770) shows the angel announcing to Sarah that she will give birth to a son. Sarah was 90 years old at the time. Tiepolo has captured Sarah's look of wonder at the news.

GOD BLESSES SARAH

Sarah was well past the age of childbearing when God told Abraham that he would be the "father of many nations." Since Sarah could not have children she allowed her servant Hagar to bear Abraham a son, who was called Ishmael. While Hagar was pregnant the two women quarreled and Sarah sent Hagar into the desert. But God appeared to Hagar and told her to return home. Several years after Ishmael was born Sarah became pregnant and gave birth to Isaac. Ishmael mocked his younger brother, so Sarah asked Abraham to banish him with his mother. She said to Abraham, "Cast out this slave woman with her son for she will never share in the inheritance with my son, Isaac."

In this 17th-century painting by the Dutch artist Fabritius Barent (1624-1673), Abraham commands Hagar and Ishmael to go into the desert of Beersheba. He has given them food and some water in a rounded pitcher but their facial expressions suggest an awareness of the danger that faces them alone in exile.

THE DISMISSAL OF HAGAR

Sarah's orders to send Ishmael and his proud mother away distressed Abraham but God told him to do as Sarah wished. So Abraham sent Hagar and Ishmael to wander in the desert. Soon their food and water ran out and Hagar feared they would die. She put Ishmael under a tree and began to cry. God saw their suffering and an angel appeared to them and said "Lift the boy and take him by the hand, for I will make him into a great nation." Then the angel showed them a well and they were saved. Ishmael became the ancestor of the 12 Arab tribes of North Africa and an important figure in the Muslim tradition.

HAGAR AND ISHMAEL
RESCUED BY AN ANGEL
Eustache Le Sueur
c. 1648
Musée des Beaux Arts, Rennes (France)

The 17th-century French painter Eustache Le Sueur (1616–1655) painted many religious works for churches in Paris. He is known for his delicate, refined colors and harmonious compositions. This painting shows Hagar (1) seated on the right with the winged angel (2) hovering above her and the baby Ishmael (3) lying almost lifeless beneath a tree. The desert of Beersheba (4) can be seen in the background, while Hagar's belongings (5) can be seen at her side.

REBEKAH AT THE WELL
Ottavio Vannini
c.1635
Kunsthistorisches Museum, Vienna
(Austria)

This work was painted by the Italian artist, Ottavio Vannini (1585–1643), who is known for his narrative scenes. In this scene, which takes place at the well in Mesopotamia, Rebekah (1) is seen pouring water from a jar into a bowl so that the servant (2), sent from Canaan by Abraham, can quench his thirst. Abraham's servant, Eliezer, traveled a long distance by camel (3) to the land of Abraham's family in search of a wife for Isaac, and he chose Rebekah because she was kind to him in giving him water to drink. In this painting there also is a group of women to the right (4) who are gathered beside the communal village well (5) to draw water and talk to each other as was the daily custom for women in those times. Rebekah soon returned with the servant to the homeland of Abraham where she joined his household and married Isaac. Many episodes from the story of Isaac and Rebekah have been depicted but the scene of the meeting of Rebekah and Eliezer is one of the most popular.

Rebekah

…Rebekah came out with her jar on her shoulder… The girl was very beautiful,… She went down to the spring, filled her jar and came up again. The servant hurried to meet her and said, "Please give me a little water from your jar." "Drink, my Lord," she said, and quickly lowered the jar to her hands and gave him a drink. **Genesis 24:15–18.**

When Abraham and Sarah's son Isaac was grown they sent their trusted servant Eliezer to Nahor, in Mesopotamia, to find a wife for him. Eliezer met Rebekah by the well and was struck by her kindness and beauty. He gave rich gifts to Rebekah's parents and she agreed to accompany him to Canaan to marry Isaac. After 20 years Rebekah gave birth to twins, Esau and Jacob. When the boys were grown Rebekah encouraged her favorite, Jacob, to deceive his father into believing he was the elder son so that he might receive his special blessing. Rebekah's deceitful actions changed the history of the Hebrew people, for she delivered their fate into the hands of the virtuous Jacob rather than into those of his brother Esau.

The Jewish Bride, by Rembrandt Van Rijn (1606-1669). God said to Rebekah, "Two nations are in your womb, and two peoples from within you will be separated; one will be stronger than the other, and the older will serve the younger" (Genesis 25:23).

ESAU AND JACOB
The twins had very different temperaments. Esau grew up to be a skillful hunter of wild game who loved life in the country, while his twin brother Jacob was a quiet, gentle boy who preferred to stay close to home. As the children matured, Rebekah grew to favor Jacob and Isaac preferred Esau.

This detail from a 12th-century mosaic at the Cathedral of Monreale, in Sicily, shows Abraham's servant Eliezer and Rebekah returning on camels to the home of Abraham. After the servant explained his mission to the family of Rebekah they agreed to let her travel with him back to Canaan to marry Isaac.

ISAAC'S BLESSING
Rebekah overheard Isaac telling Esau that he would soon die and he would give him the blessing due to a first son. While Esau was out hunting, Rebekah called Jacob and advised him to fetch some game and prepare food to please his father. In the meantime, she prepared goatskin for Jacob to wear on his hands so that when he approached his father he would trick him into believing that he was his hairier brother. When Jacob brought the food to his father, Isaac did not recognize him. He said, "The voice is the voice of Jacob, but the hands are the hands of Esau," and he gave him his blessing.

This detail from a fresco by Giotto (1267–1337) in St. Francis Basilica at Assisi (Italy), shows Esau who has returned with food to receive his father's blessing. Isaac was forced to refuse him.

Rachel and Leah

When Jacob met Rachel at the well he kissed her and started to weep out of joy.

Now Laban had two daughters; the name of the older was Leah, and the name of the younger was Rachel.... Jacob was in love with Rachel and said (to Laban) "I'll work for you seven years in return for your younger daughter Rachel.... So Jacob served seven years to get Rachel, but they seemed like only a few days to him because of his love for her.
Genesis 31:16–20

JACOB

Jacob fled his home to escape the wrath of his brother Esau whom he had cheated (see page 11). When Jacob reached the well of Haran he met Rachel and told her he was Rebekah's son. Rachel ran to tell her father and Jacob was a guest in their house.

This painting by the Dutch artist Hendrick ter Brugghen (1588–1629), shows Jacob confronting Laban the day after the wedding. At the end of the week-long celebrations for his marriage to Leah, Jacob was granted the right to marry Rachel too.

Rachel met Jacob at a village well, just as Eliezer had met Jacob's mother Rebekah. Jacob fell in love with her, and her father, Laban, promised Rachel to him in exchange for seven years work. But, when the seven years were up, Laban tricked Jacob into marrying her older sister Leah. Jacob eventually married Rachel too, but he had to work for seven more years. Leah bore Jacob six sons and a daughter. Rachel had two sons – Joseph and Benjamin. Each of their sons was the ancestor of one of the Twelve Tribes of Israel.

RACHEL AND LEAH FLEE WITH JACOB

For many years after their marriage, Rachel and Leah did not get along well. Leah had many children, but Rachel was always Jacob's favorite. The two women were united, however, in agreeing to leave their father and to return to Jacob's homeland in Canaan. When they left Rachel stole her father's idols. Laban came after them and demanded that the idols be returned to him. Jacob, who knew nothing of the theft, assured Laban that whoever had stolen should be punished by death.

Tiepolo's painting shows Laban angrily demanding the return of his idols. Rachel had hidden them beneath her saddle and Laban did not discover them. Rachel died in child birth soon after. Jacob erected a pillar on her grave. Rachel's grave is still visible today, just outside of Bethlehem.

RACHEL HIDING THE IDOLS STOLEN FROM HER FATHER

Giovanni Battista Tiepolo
1726–9
Palazzo Arcivescovile, Udine, (Italy)

This fresco by the Italian master Giovanni Battista Tiepolo (1696–1770) was painted for the Archbishop's palace in Udine, in northern Italy. It shows Rachel (1) sitting on her father's teraphim, or small idols, hidden beneath a camel's saddle (2). The elderly Laban (3) raises his hands to remonstrate with Rachel and appears to plead for the safe return of his idols while Jacob (4) looks on. The action takes place in a tent (5) with camels (6) in the background. Leah (7) and Jacob's children (8) by both Rachel and Leah are also shown in the tent.

MOSES SAVED FROM THE WATERS
Orazio Gentileschi
1630–33
Prado, Madrid (Spain)

The Italian painter, Orazio Gentileschi (1562-1647), known for his graceful figures and refined chiaroscuro style, created this painting. It shows the pharaoh's daughter (1) in 17th-century costume surrounded by her elegantly dressed hand-maids (2), pointing at the basket before her which contains the baby Moses (3). In the left foreground Miriam (4) kneels and makes a gesture of entreaty as she presents Jochebed (5), Moses' mother, to the pharaoh's daughter as a wet nurse. The pharaoh's daughter paid Jochebed to nurse the baby. After three years, she returned him to be raised in the pharaoh's court. The Nile River (6), which carried Moses to the pharaoh's daughter, flows past in the background.

JOCHEBED SETS MOSES ADRIFT

Jochebed hid Moses for three months. When she could no longer hide him she put him in a reed basket and set it adrift on the waters of the Nile River. Miriam followed the basket from a distance to keep a watchful eye over the baby and observed the finding of the basket and child by the pharaoh's daughter. Thanks to the intercession of Miriam, Jochebed was later reunited with Moses because her daughter suggested that she should be employed as the baby's wet nurse for three years. After three years Moses was returned to the pharaoh's daughter who raised him as an Egyptian prince in the pharaoh's court.

Jochebed and Miriam

The Pharaoh's daughter went down to the Nile to bathe,…. She saw the basket among the reeds and sent her slave girl to get it. She opened it and saw the baby… Then his sister asked Pharaoh's daughter, "Shall I go and get one of the Hebrew women to nurse the baby for you?" "Yes, go," she answered. And the girl went and got the baby's mother. Exodus 2:5–8

Jochebed was the mother of Moses. Her story takes place in Egypt, at a time when the Israelites, or Hebrews, were enslaved. When the pharaoh gave an order that all newborn Hebrew male children should be killed, Jochebed hid her son for three months and then allowed him to be raised by another woman to save his life. Miriam was Moses' sister. She helped to save her brother when he was a baby, and was also known as a prophetess who aided Moses in leading the Hebrews out of Egypt.

This painting by the Pre-Raphaelite artist Simeon Solomon (1840–1905) shows Jochebed and Miriam looking lovingly at the baby Moses before they put him in the reed basket that was placed on the Nile.

THE MIDWIVES

Two other women tried to save Moses and the other Hebrew baby boys. These were Shiprah and Puah, midwives to the Hebrew women. Although the pharaoh instructed them to kill all the Hebrews' firstborn sons they did not do so. When the pharaoh asked them why they disobeyed him they replied by saying "Hebrew women are not like Egyptian women; they are vigorous and give birth before the midwives arrive" (Exodus 1:19).

Jochebed set the baby Moses adrift on the waters of the Nile River to save him from the pharaoh's order.

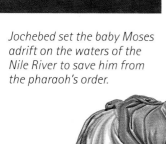

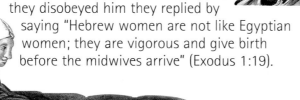

This illustration from a Spanish Golden Haggadah of the 14th century, shows Miriam with other women as they dance and play music to celebrate the destruction of the pharaoh's army in the Red Sea.

MIRIAM'S SONG

The Hebrews were enslaved by the Egyptians for hundreds of years. When Moses became an adult, he learned of his true identity and was called by God to free his people and to lead them out of Egypt. Moses led them to the Red Sea which he then caused to part and let his people walk through. When the Egyptians followed, the waters fell back and drowned them. Upon seeing this, Miriam took a tambourine in her hand and all the women joyfully followed her, singing and dancing to praise God for delivering them from the pharaoh's army.

Deborah and Jael

...the Israelites once again did evil in the eyes of the Lord. So the Lord sold them into the hands of Jabin, a king of Canaan.... The commander of his army was Sisera... (who) cruelly oppressed the Israelites for twenty years.... Deborah, a prophetess... was leading Israel at that time. She held court under the Palm of Deborah... and the Israelites came to her to have their disputes settled. **Judges 4:1–5**

Deborah is a unique figure in the Bible. She is the only female Judge, or political leader, of the Israelite tribes in Palestine prior to the establishment of a unified kingdom. During her rule, oppression by the Canaanites became intolerable and she decided to rise up against them. Deborah's faith in God was such that she mounted an attack and won, despite the Canaanites much stronger army, and the fact that her own general, Barak, was unsure of victory. Deborah also prophesied that it would be a woman — Jael — who would kill the Canaanite general Sisera at the end of the battle.

This Baroque statue from Aix-en-Provence, France shows Deborah holding a victory torch. Before she became a warrior, Deborah was a Judge who used her wisdom to solve disputes among the Israelites.

This illustration from a 13th-century French Bible shows Deborah riding with Barak in a horse-drawn chariot. She is gesturing forward toward Mount Tabor where Sisera and his army met defeat.

DEBORAH SUMMONS BARAK

According to the Old Testament book of Judges (4–5), the Israelites had found disfavor in the eyes of God and so he allowed Sisera, the cruel general of a Canaanite king called Jabin, to oppress them for 20 years. Sisera's army, with its "900 iron chariots," discouraged the Israelites from rebelling. Deborah sent for Barak, an Israelite general, and told him that God commanded him to take 10,000 men to Mount Tabor to defeat Sisera and his army. Barak refused to lead the army unless Deborah went with him. Deborah agreed to go but told him that, because of his reluctance to act, the final honor of killing Sisera would be given to a woman.

JAEL AND SISERA

Sisera's army was defeated as predicted by Deborah and Sisera sought refuge by fleeing to the tent of Jael, the wife of Heber the Kenite. According to the Bible, Sisera fled to the tent of Jael because there were friendly relations between the king of Sisera's people, Jabin, and the clan of Jael's husband. She offered him hospitality, but instead of protecting him, she murdered him by driving a tent peg into his head while he was asleep. Once again Deborah's prophecy was fulfilled.

This detail from a painting by Italian painter Ottavio Vannini (1585–1643) shows Jael as she drives the tent peg into Sisera's head.

JAEL REVEALS SISERA'S BODY
Donato Creti
c.1730
Banca Popolare, Milan (Italy)

The Italian artist Donato Creti (1671–1749), a leading painter of Bologna during the 18th century, depicted this dramatic scene. Jael (1), who is dressed in long flowing robes, can be seen pulling open her tent (2) inviting Barak (3) inside to reveal to him the body of Sisera (4), whom she has just killed. The lethal tent peg (5) which she has used to murder the general sticks out of his forehead. Outside her tent, the bodies of Sisera's defeated soldiers (6) are lying on the ground as victorious soldiers (7) march by. The use of rich colors and the strong contrast between light and dark in this painting are typical of Baroque paintings. Creti came out of the Bolognese school which was led by the Carracci family during the early 16th century, and later by Guido Reni (1575–1642).

JEPHTHAH'S DAUGHTER

Jephthah, like Samson, was an Israelite warrior and Judge. On the eve of an important battle he promised God that in return for victory he would sacrifice the first creature that emerged from the door of his house when he came home from battle. On his return, his daughter, an only child, came out to greet him. Bound to his pact, Jephthah allowed his daughter to roam the hills for two months with her friends before sacrificing her to God.

The tragic moment showing the daughter of Jephthah stepping out joyfully from their home to greet her victorious father. As in this engraving, Jephthah's daughter is usually shown with a tambourine as she dances out the door.

Delilah and Jephthah's Daughter

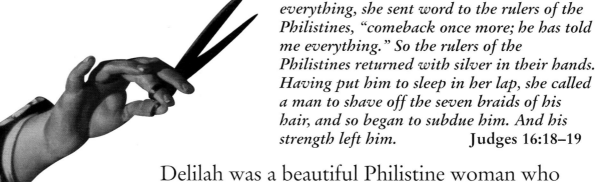

When Delilah saw that he had told her everything, she sent word to the rulers of the Philistines, "comeback once more; he has told me everything." So the rulers of the Philistines returned with silver in their hands. Having put him to sleep in her lap, she called a man to shave off the seven braids of his hair, and so began to subdue him. And his strength left him. **Judges 16:18–19**

According to the Bible's account, Delilah called a man to shave Samson's braids. In artistic tradition, however, Delilah is usually depicted holding scissors or actually cutting Samson's hair.

Delilah was a beautiful Philistine woman who betrayed Samson, a heroic Judge of Israel. Her actions delivered Samson into the hands of his enemies. The daughter of Jephthah was the innocent and loyal child of another great Israelite Judge and warrior whose life was sacrificed to God. Jephthah's daughter is remembered for her strength in accepting her fate.

DELILAH BETRAYS SAMSON

Samson fell in love with Delilah and the rulers of the Philistines offered her a great deal of money if she could discover the secret of Samson's strength. Samson gave her various false explanations but finally revealed the truth to her; his strength lay in the length of his hair. She betrayed him to the Philistines while he was sleeping beside her. His hair was cut off and he lost his strength, thus enabling the Philistines to blind and imprison him in Gaza.

SAMSON AND DELILAH

Matthias Stom
c.1630
Galleria Nazionale d'Arte
Antica, Rome (Italy)

Matthias Stom (1600–1650) was a 17th-century Dutch painter who received his training in Utrecht. He painted in the style of the Italian master Michelangelo Merisi da Caravaggio (1571–1610). In this painting the body of Samson (1) is in the foreground of the composition. Delilah (2) holds a pair of scissors (3) and is clearly about to cut Samson's hair. Beside her an old woman (4) watches and raises an admonishing finger. A Philistine soldier (5) stands and watches on the left. The figures are all strongly lit by candlelight to the left of the composition, creating accentuated shadows, typical of the Caravaggesque style. As in many paintings of the time, the figures are dressed in contemporary clothes.

DELILAH, THE PHILISTINE

Delilah, whose name has become synonymous with treachery, was a Philistine. The Philistines settled in southern Palestine in about 1200 BC and fought with the Israelites for the land. Delilah is unusual in the Bible because she acts alone to destroy an enemy of her people. She is also referred to by name and not in relation to males, as was usual at the time.

This painting by Rembrandt van Rijn (1606–1669) shows Samson having his eyes gouged by the Philistines while Delilah runs away with scissors in one hand and locks of Samson's hair in the other.

An example of Philistine pottery believed to represent a fertility goddess or a birthing chair. Very little is known of Philistine religion, but scholars believe that their gods were borrowed from the Canaanites they conquered.

THE SUMMER OF RUTH AND BOAZ
Nicolas Poussin
1660–1664
Louvre, Paris
(France)

The French artist Nicolas Poussin (1594–1665) spent most of his working life painting in Rome. This pastoral scene by Poussin depicts Ruth (1), seen here on her knees, before Boaz (2), the wealthy owner of the land (3). She entreats him to allow her to glean (collect) the grain (4) left on the ground after the harvest. Boaz had heard about all she had done for Naomi and was kind to her. He ordered his men not to harass her as she worked in the fields to gather grain.

Ruth and Hannah

…Naomi said, "Return home, my daughters. Why should you come with me?…" … But Ruth replied, "Don't urge me to leave you or to turn back from you. Where you go I will go, and where you stay I will stay. Your people will be my people and your God my God. Where you die I will die and there I will be buried." **Ruth 1:11–17**

The lives of Ruth and Hannah epitomize traditional values and roles for women such as loyalty and dedicated motherhood. Ruth's refusal to leave Naomi, quoted above, is a testament to her loyalty. Her selfless devotion to her mother-in-law makes her one of the best-loved women in the Old Testament. Hannah prayed for many years before she was granted a son. At last, she gave birth to Samuel, whom she raised with such care that he became the last and the greatest of the Judges of Israel.

RUTH CARES FOR NAOMI

Ruth, a Moabite woman, married a Hebrew man living in Moab. When Ruth's husband died, her mother-in-law Naomi, also a widow, decided to return to her native Bethlehem. She told Ruth to return to her family, but Ruth insisted on accompanying Naomi to Bethlehem. Ruth's determination is noteworthy since it was particularly dangerous in those times for two women to travel alone. They had little money and Ruth took on the most humble tasks to provide for Naomi and herself.

This detail from an illustration by William Blake (1757-1827) shows Ruth embracing Naomi as she refuses to leave.

RUTH AND BOAZ

In Bethlehem the word about Ruth's devotion to Naomi and her diligence quickly spread. A rich and respected farmer named Boaz, a relative of Naomi, fell in love with her and married her. Ruth and Boaz eventually became the parents of Obed who was the grandfather of David, the second king of Israel.

HANNAH

Although grief-stricken by her inability to have a child, Hannah never lost her faith in God. She went on praying and believing, and vowed that if she had a child she would dedicate him to God. After many years, God heard her prayer and she gave birth to the prophet and Judge Samuel whom she raised with wisdom and love.

Right: An illuminated page from a French 13th-century Book of Ruth shows Boaz, Ruth, and their children. According to the Bible, Naomi cared for Obed, Ruth's first born child, as one of her own.

Far left: This illustration shows Hannah praying with the priest Eli in the background. When he saw Hannah praying he was moved by her faithful devotion and blessed her.

Bathsheba

One evening David got up from his bed and walked around on the roof of the palace. From the roof he saw a woman bathing. The woman was very beautiful and David sent someone to find out about her. The man said "Isn't this Bathsheba, the daughter of Eliam and the wife of Uriah the Hittite?" 2 Samuel 11:2-3

DAVID AND BATHSHEBA
Lucas Cranach the Elder.
1526
Kunsthistorisches Museum, Vienna (Austria)

Lucas Cranach (1472-1553) was a German painter of great skill and originality who did many works with religious and mythological subjects. In this painting, Bathsheba (1) is the seated figure being bathed out in the open by her three maidservants (2) while King David (3), who has gotten up from his bed, watches her from above from the balcony of his beautiful royal palace (4). David is playing a harp (5) to attract the attention of Bathsheba and he uses this traditional instrument to make her fall in love with him. She is aware of his gaze and her body is turned toward him as her bare feet and legs are being washed. The elaborate dresses, hats, and jewelry worn by the Bathsheba and her maid servants were typical adornments of wealthy ladies in Germany at the time Cranach was painting. The hill village in the background (6) is also a typical northern European landscape of the period.

Bathsheba was the beautiful wife of a Hittite general named Uriah. When the Hebrew king David saw her bathing he was so struck by her beauty that he fell in love and wanted to marry her. David arranged to have her husband put into the front line of battle where the fighting was fiercest so he would be sure to die, leaving Bathsheba free to remarry. Bathsheba played a passive role in this treacherous episode, and later emerges as one of the most influential women at the king's court, ensuring that her son Solomon should succeed David on the throne.

BATHSHEBA AND KING DAVID

When David fell in love with Bathsheba he knew that he could not have her as his wife because she was married to Uriah, one of his most trusted Hittite generals. At the time, Uriah was fighting with David's army against the Ammonites. David invited him to the royal palace, allegedly to discuss the progress of the war. The king sent him back to war with a sealed letter addressed to Joab, the army commander, which arranged for Uriah to meet certain death in the front line of battle. God was angry with David for this piece of treachery and as punishment David and Bathsheba's first child died. They had four other sons, including Solomon, who became a great Hebrew king.

During the Middle Ages it was not unusual to depict biblical scenes in contemporary settings. This Flemish tapestry shows Bathsheba and King David in the royal court, surrounded by lords and ladies, dressed in typical medieval costume.

This illustration from an illuminated manuscript shows Bathsheba kneeling before her son, Solomon, who once anointed king, gave her the power and authority as queen mother.

BATHSHEBA SECURES SOLOMON'S RIGHT TO THE THRONE

When David was old and dying there was some dispute over which son would succeed him. The prophet Nathan, whose respect she must have won, informed Bathsheba of a plot by one of David's other son's, Adonijah, to become the future king. Bathsheba, as a prominent and powerful figure at court, quickly took action. She made sure that her son, Solomon (who was younger than his older half brothers, and therefore had a lesser claim to the throne), became king of Israel after David's death. According to biblical tradition Bathsheba was David's favorite wife, and when she visited the aged king she heard her plea. She told him about Adonijah's plot and the king then said to her, "Solomon your son shall be king after me, and he will sit on my throne in my place" (1 Kings 1:30). David then ordered his priest to anoint Solomon. Solomon became the legendary and most wise king of Israel.

·j·5·Z·8·

The Queen of Sheba

When the queen of Sheba heard about the fame of Solomon..., she came to test him with hard questions. Arriving at Jerusalem with a very great caravan... she came to Solomon and talked with him about all that she had on her mind. ... When the queen of Sheba saw all the wisdom of Solomon and the palace he had built... she was overwhelmed. **1 Kings 10:1–5**

The Queen of Sheba was the beautiful, exotic queen of Sheba (or Saba), now modern-day Yemen in southwest Arabia. She made a very famous visit to King Solomon's court and arrived in Jerusalem with a huge caravan of camels laden with gold, jewels, and spices. The reason for her visit was probably to promote good business relations between Arabia and Israel, which were essential to preserve the lucrative trade routes that linked Arabia to important markets in Palestine and Mesopotamia.

This limestone statue from ancient Yemen shows a woman wearing a diadem (crown) and beaded necklaces.

THE QUEEN OF SHEBA ARRIVING AT THE COURT OF KING SOLOMON
Apollonio di Giovanni di Tommaso
c.1450
Agnew & Sons Gallery, London (England)

The Italian artist Apollonio di Giovanni di Tommaso (1417-65) painted this panel that once decorated the front of a large wooden chest which may have contained a bride's dowry. The painting shows the Queen of Sheba (1) arriving at the court of King Solomon under a royal canopy (2). The camels in her caravan are laden down with chests (3) containing gifts for Solomon as they cross a bridge (4). The king's palace (5) is visible in the background.

THE QUEEN OF SHEBA IN SOLOMON'S KINGDOM

In the biblical account, the Queen of Sheba's visit to Solomon's court was a magnificent occasion. She visited him with her lavish caravan of gifts in order to test his legendary wisdom with a series of riddles. In return, Solomon gave her "all she desired and asked for, besides what he had given her out of his royal bounty" (1 Kings 10:13). The Queen of Sheba was an exceptional woman because she traveled a long distance to find out for herself about Solomon's renowned wisdom and boldly set her wits and riches against those of Solomon. She is a fine example of female independence and resourcefulness in biblical times.

KING SOLOMON AND THE TWO MOTHERS

In another story involving women during Solomon's reign, two mothers gave birth at the same time. One of the babies died and both women claimed the remaining child as her own. Solomon, using his legendary wisdom, discovered the identity of the real mother by offering to slice the child in half so they could each have half. The real mother refused and Solomon recognized that she was showing the emotions of a true, loving mother who would rather loose her child than see him die (see 1 Kings 3).

This painting by the Italian Renaissance artist Raphael (1483–1520), shows the reaction of the true mother as one of Solomon's men prepares to slice the infant in half.

In this painting by the Flemish painter Frans Francken the Elder (1542-1615), Solomon sits resplendent on his magnificent throne to receive the kneeling Queen of Sheba who lays out her fabulous gifts of gold, jewels, and spices before him.

Susanna and Judith

This detail from a painting by Jacopo da Empoli (1554-1640) shows Susanna sending her maidservants into the house to bring her oil and ointments which leaves her briefly alone in her enclosed garden.

She went up to the post at the end of the bed, above Holofernes' head, and took down the sword that hung there…. And she struck his neck twice with all her might and severed it from his body…after a moment she went out and gave Holofernes' head to her maid, who placed it in her food bag. Then the two of them went out together, … and they passed through the camp and circled around the valley and went up the mountain to Bethulia and came to its gates. **Judith 13:4-10**

The stories of Susanna and Judith are excluded from many modern editions, both Protestant and Jewish, of the Bible, but they are included in the Roman Catholic and Orthodox canons. For artists, they are popular subjects that have inspired many fine works of art. Susanna was the beautiful and virtuous wife of Joachim, who courageously faced false accusations and a death sentence. Judith was a beautiful widow who saved her hometown, Bethulia, from Assyrian invasion by decapitating the general of the Assyrian army.

SUSANNA AND THE PROPHET DANIEL

Two elders in the community secretly desired Susanna and sought to make trouble for her. They watched her bathing alone in her beautiful garden and approached her. When she spurned their attentions, they took revenge by falsely accusing her of betraying her husband. She was brought before the Jewish court and was unjustly found guilty and sentenced to death. Daniel, the young prophet sent by God to save her, cross-examined the villainous elders and revealed their false witness and Susanna's innocence.

In this painting by the Italian painter Sebastiano Ricci (1659-1734), Daniel gestures towards the virtuous Susanna. The artist convincingly manages to convey Susanna's anxiety, fear, and shame.

The relief carving on this 12th-century French backgammon piece shows Judith in the act of slicing Holofernes' head off as he lies sleeping on a four poster bed. This scene has been widely depicted by artists.

JUDITH AND HOLOFERNES

The army of Holofernes, an Assyrian general, laid siege to the Jewish city of Bethulia. To prevent the city from capitulating to the enemy, Judith, a beautiful and virtuous widow, crossed into the enemy camp intending to meet Holofernes and save her city. Having gained the trust of Holofernes by claiming to betray her own people to him, she cut off his head with his own sword, as he lay sleeping in a drunken stupor. The public display of his decapitated head caused the Assyrians to flee their camp the next morning and Bethulia and its inhabitants were saved.

JUDITH WITH THE HEAD OF HOLOFERNES
Sandro Botticelli
c. 1472
Uffizi Gallery, Florence (Italy)

Sandro Botticelli (1445–1510) was an Italian painter who lived and worked in Florence. In the foreground of this painting, he has shown Judith (1) and her maid (2) fleeing from the Assyrian camp. The maid is carrying Holofernes' head (3) in a basket on her head, while Judith holds Holofernes' sword (4). She also carries an olive branch (5) as a symbol of the peace she has brought to her people. In the background, a second, much smaller scene (6) shows Holofernes' head displayed on the city walls while the Israelites emerge from the city gates, putting the Assyrian army to flight. Behind the main action a Flemish-style landscape (7) stretches away into the background. The painting also reminds us how Renaissance artists treated biblical subjects with considerable freedom: Judith's flight took place at night, but here the heroine and her maid are bathed in the clear light of day.

Esther

Purim Scroll of the Book of Esther.

Esther put on her royal robes and stood in the inner court of the palace, in front of the King's hall. The King was sitting on his royal throne in the hall, facing the entrance. When he saw the Queen Esther standing in the court, he was pleased with her and held out the gold scepter that was in his hand.
Esther 5:1-2

Esther was a lovely young Hebrew woman who was raised as an adopted daughter by her cousin Mordecai. King Ahasuerus chose her to be his wife and she married him without revealing her Hebrew origins. As queen she is famous for prevailing upon Ahasuerus to save her people from the murderous designs of Haman, a prominent court official who disliked Israelites. When Haman sent instructions throughout the kingdom to kill all Israelites, Esther bravely approached the king to intercede and appeal on behalf of her people. Although nobody was allowed to approach the king unannounced, the king accepted her and agreed to meet with her and Haman.

A portrait of Esther by the Italian artist Andrea del Castagno (1421–57). According to the Book of Esther, *she "won the favor of everyone who saw her."*

ESTHER, QUEEN OF PERSIA

Esther was chosen as queen of Persia by Ahasuerus (the historical King Xerxes, 486–465 BC) to replace his former wife Vashti. The king, who was a capricious man, had deposed Vashti because she refused an order to appear before him at a party. Esther was justifiably frightened of entering the king's presence unannounced but persisted because she wished to save her people. The annual Jewish Festival of Purim celebrates her courage and single-mindedness.

Left: This painting by the Dutch artist Jan Lievens (1607–74), shows Esther, the king, and Haman seated at the banquet at the moment when Esther reveals Haman's plot. The king clenches his fists in anger as Haman draws back in fear.

THE BANQUET

Upon her acceptance into the king's throne room, Esther invited Ahasuerus to join her and Haman at a banquet. While the three of them were dining the king turned to Esther and said, "Queen Esther, what is your petition? It will be given you. What is your request? Even up to half the kingdom, it will be granted." Esther revealed Haman's plot to murder the Jews. The king became furious and left the table. Haman feared for his life and begged Esther to save him, throwing himself at her on the couch where she lay. The king returned at just that moment and was further angered. He had Haman hanged and countermanded his orders to kill the Jews.

ESTHER BEFORE AHASUERUS

Pompeo Girolamo Batoni
c. 1765
Philadelphia Museum of Art (USA)

In this painting by the Italian painter Pompeo Girolamo Batoni (1708–1787), the Jewish heroine Esther (1) is depicted with her maidservants (2) entering the presence of her husband, the Persian king, Ahasuerus (3) who is seated on his throne at his splendid court. Even as his wife, she was forbidden to enter the king's presence without being summoned. Entering the king's presence without permission was punishable by death. But the courageous Esther, dressed in her finest clothes, was determined to approach the king to save her people. In this scene she swoons with relief as the king signals with his golden scepter (4) that he will condone her intrusion and receive her. As the story reveals, she then proceeds to plead with him to stop the slaughter of all the Israelites in the Persian Empire. Esther's determination in the face of danger earned her the reputation of a national savior. Thanks to her intercession the king issued an edict which granted all Jews in every city the right to assemble and protect themselves.

Old Testament Women

Bathsheba: the beautiful wife of Uriah the Hittite, she later married King David and was the mother of King Solomon.

Deborah: the only woman among the Old Testament Judges, she prophesied that the Canaanite general Sisera would be killed by a woman.

Delilah: betrayed Samson to the Philistines by revealing that the secret of his strength lay in his hair.

Esther: wife of King Ahasuerus who interceded on behalf of the Jewish people to save them from a murderous plot.

Eve: the first woman, was created as a companion for Adam in the Garden of Eden. She is known as the mother of all humans.

Hagar: the servant of Sarah and mother of Ishmael who was cast out into the desert with her son and later saved by an angel.

Hannah: barren after many years of marriage, she prayed to God for a son and became the mother of Samuel, prophet, priest, and Judge.

Jael: the wife of Heber the Kenite who murdered Sisera by driving a tent peg into his head.

Jephthah's Daughter: was sacrificed because of a pact her father made with God in exchange for military victory.

Jochebed: the mother of Moses and Miriam. She placed Moses in a reed basket in the Nile River to save him from death.

Judith: a beautiful widow from Bethulia who cut off the head of the Assyrian general Holofernes so that her city could be saved.

Leah: daughter of Laban who allowed her father to trick Joseph into marrying her when he thought he was marrying Rachel.

Miriam: the daughter of Jochebed, she followed and watched over the reed basket containing the baby Moses as it floated down the Nile River.

Queen of Sheba: visited King Solomon's court with a caravan of camels carrying gifts of gold, jewelry, and spices.

Rachel: beloved wife of Jacob, who worked for 14 years for the privilege of marrying her.

Rebekah: wife of Isaac and mother of Jacob and Esau, who helped Jacob deceive his father into giving him the blessing that was due to Esau.

Ruth: a young widow who accompanied her mother-in-law Naomi to Bethlehem. There she met and married Boaz.

Sarah: wife of Abraham, mother of Isaac. She persuaded Abraham to cast out Hagar and Ishmael into the desert.

Susanna: virtuous wife of Joachim who was watched while bathing by two elders in her community and falsely accused. She was saved by the prophet Daniel.

Eve

Judith

Queen of Sheba

Susanna

Esther

Hagar

Jochebed and Miriam

Rachel

Rebekah

Artists' Biographies

Apollonio di Giovanni di Tommaso (born c. 1415, died 1465, Florence) was a manuscript illuminator, painter, and member of the artists' guild in Florence. Specializing in works for domestic settings, most of his patrons were merchants, bankers, and notaries. Together with Marco del Buono (1402–1489), also known as Giamberti, he ran the most successful shop for decorating trunks in Florence from around 1446.

Pompeo Batoni (born 1708, Lucca, died 1787, Rome), an Italian painter and draftsman who was active in Rome, where he settled in 1727. He has been described as the last great Italian personality to dominate painting in Rome. Initially he made his name with exquisite drawings of ancient statuary, then as a history painter, mainly of religious subjects. However, by the 1750's he was devoting most of his time to portraits and it is for these that he is principally famous. At the time of his death he was probably the most famous artist in Europe, but his reputation went into eclipse in the 19th century and was not revived until the end of the 20th century.

Hieronymus Bosch (born c.1450 's-Hertogenbosch, died 1516, 's-Hertogenbosch) was a Dutch painter active for all his known career in his native town. Although it was fairly remote from the major art centers of Flanders, it had a vigorous cultural and intellectual life. His paintings have an extraordinarily vivid imaginative power and are full of symbols, but the basic themes are often quite simple. Many of his subjects came from the popular culture of his age, notably proverbs and devotional literature. More than half his paintings are of traditional Christian subjects, and others deal with moral themes, often illustrating human greed and folly.

Sandro Botticelli (born 1445, Florence, died 1510, Florence), whose real name was Alessandro di Mariano Filipepi, was a Renaissance painter best known for his paintings of mythological subjects, such as

The Birth of Venus and *The Primavera*. He received commissions from the Medici family and major churches. In 1481 he was called to Rome, along with other artists, to paint the walls of the Sistine Chapel in the Vatican. During the later years of his career, Botticelli turned to small-scale paintings and is believed to have taken many stylistic elements from northern European painters.

Lucas Cranach the Elder (born 1472, Kronach, died 1553, Weimar) was a German painter and designer of woodcuts. Very little is known of his life before he moved to Vienna in about 1501 where he worked for the humanist circles associated with the university. His stay in Vienna was brief, but in this period he painted some of his finest and most original works. Cranach moved to Wittenberg as court painter to Frederick III, Elector of Saxony in 1542, where he remained until 1550. He then followed the Elector John Frederick into exile, to Augsburg, Innsbruck, and finally Weimar. During his time in Wittenberg he became extremely wealthy and one of the most respected citizens.

Donato Creti (born 1671, Cremona, died 1749, Bologna) was apprenticed to Giorgio Raparini (1660–1725) in Bologna. His talent was soon noted and he moved to the studio of Lorenzo Pasinelli (1629–1700), the leading Bolognese painter of that time. Around 1700 he traveled to Venice where he saw the works of Veronese (1528–88) and Titian (1488–1576), two artists whose work he greatly admired. He painted many mythological and pastoral subjects for Bolognese nobles and Roman cardinals. During the latter part of his career he turned to religious subects.

Orazio Gentileschi (born 1563, Pisa, died 1639, England) was an Italian painter who settled in Rome in 1576 and became one of the closest and most gifted followers of Caravaggio (1571–1610). In 1621 he moved to Genoa, where he stayed until 1623. After working for Marie de' Medici in Paris, he settled in England in 1626 and became

court painter to Charles I. He was held in great esteem in England and stayed there until his death. His travels helped to spread the Caravaggesque style. His daughter Artemisia Gentileschi (1593–c.1652) was also a painter.

Eustache Le Sueur (born 1616, Paris, died 1655, Paris) was active throughout his career in Paris. In the 1640's he was profoundly affected by the paintings of Poussin and his work became more classical as a result. In the last years of his life his chief model became Raphael, especially the engravings of his tapestry designs. Le Sueur was a founder member of the French *Académie Royale* in 1648. In his own day he was almost as well thought of as Poussin, and in the 18th century he was known as "the French Raphael," but his reputation declined in the 19th century and he is now considered a minor master.

Nicolas Poussin (born 1594, Les Andelys, died 1665, Rome), a French painter, spent the most part of his career in Rome. There he met many influential people and studied classical art (a style modeled after the art of ancient Greece and Rome). He became one of the greatest painters in Rome at the time. He went to France in 1638 where he served King Louis XIII as court painter for two years. He then returned to Rome and during the later period of his career painted scenes from classical mythology and the Bible. Poussin's style inspired many artists who called themselves Poussinists; they believed that form was more important than color in art.

Matthias Stom or Stomer (born c.1600, Amersfoort, died c.1650, Sicily), was a Dutch painter who worked for most of his active life in Italy. The details of his life are obscure, but he was one of the most prolific and committed followers of Caravaggio. He worked in Rome in the 1630's, moved to Naples a few years later, and from about 1640 he lived in Sicily. There are about 200 surviving pictures by him, mainly religious works but also some mythological and genre

scenes. They are remarkable for their psychological intensity and their distinctive clay-like treatment of flesh.

Giovanni Battista Tiepolo (born 1696, Venice, died 1770, Madrid) was an extremely productive Italian painter and draftsman. His pictures are full of action with figures and objects seen in a deep, theatrical perspective. Tiepolo's work was always underpinned by superb draftsmanship which allowed him to depict figures soaring overhead so fluently and convincingly, particularly in his ceiling frescoes. In 1726–8 Tiepolo carried out his first major work outside Venice, the decoration of the Archbishop's Palace in Udine, and this led to a string of commissions. By 1736 his fame was such that he was invited to Stockholm to decorate the Royal Palace, an invitation he declined.

Ottavio Vannini (born 1584, Florence, died 1644, Florence) was an Italian painter who studied with Domenico Passignano (1558–1638). Influenced by the work of Michelangelo and Raphael, he developed a personal style based on 16th century classicism. His most important patron was Andrea del Rosso for whom he painted some frescoes for his private chapel in Florence. *Rebekah at the Well* is considered one of his finest paintings.

Konrad Witz (born 1400, Rottweil, died 1444, Basel) came from Swabia (in modern Germany) but spent most of his working life in Basel, Switzerland. Like most artists of his time, Witz concentrated on religious subjects, producing a number of altarpieces and devotional paintings. His style was close to that of the Flemish painters Jan van Eyck, Rogier van der Weyden, and Petrus Christus, with whom he shared a liking for showing vast landscapes populated with tiny episodes drawn from everyday life and contemporary architecture. Many critics consider his *Miraculous Draught of Fishes*, with its depiction of Lake Geneva, to be the first European painting to portray an actual landscape rather than an idealized setting.

Index

Acknowledgments

The Publishers would like to thank the following photographers and picture libraries for the photos used in this book.
Artothek, Spezialarchiv für Gemäldefotografie, Weilheim: 5, 19 center
Corbis / Contrasto, Milan: 1, 10-11, 12 bottom, 18-19, 25 bottom left, 26 top, 28 bottom, 28-29
Electa Mondadori, Milan: 11 center, 17
The Bridgeman Art Library / Farabola Foto, Milan: 8 center, 9, 15 top, 21 bottom, 23, 24-25 top
Scala Group, Florence: cover, 2, 3, 4 top, 4 bottom, 6-7, 12-13, 14-15, 16 center, 20-21, 22 center, 26 top, 26 center, 27